NORFOLK
ABOVE & BEYOND

A VIEW OF THE COUNTY FROM INTERNATIONALLY ACCLAIMED AERIAL PHOTOGRAPHER

MARTIN W. BOWMAN

HALSGROVE

First published in Great Britain in 2007
Copyright text and pictures © 2007 Martin W. Bowman

British Library Cataloguing-in-Publication Data
A CIP record for this title is available from the
British Library

ISBN 978 1 84114 591 4

HALSGROVE
Halsgrove House
Ryelands Farm Industrial Estate, Bagley Green,
Wellington, Somerset TA21 9PZ
T: 01823 653777
F: 01823 216796
email: sales@halsgrove.com
website: www.halsgrove.com

Printed and bound by D'Auria Industrie Grafiche, Italy

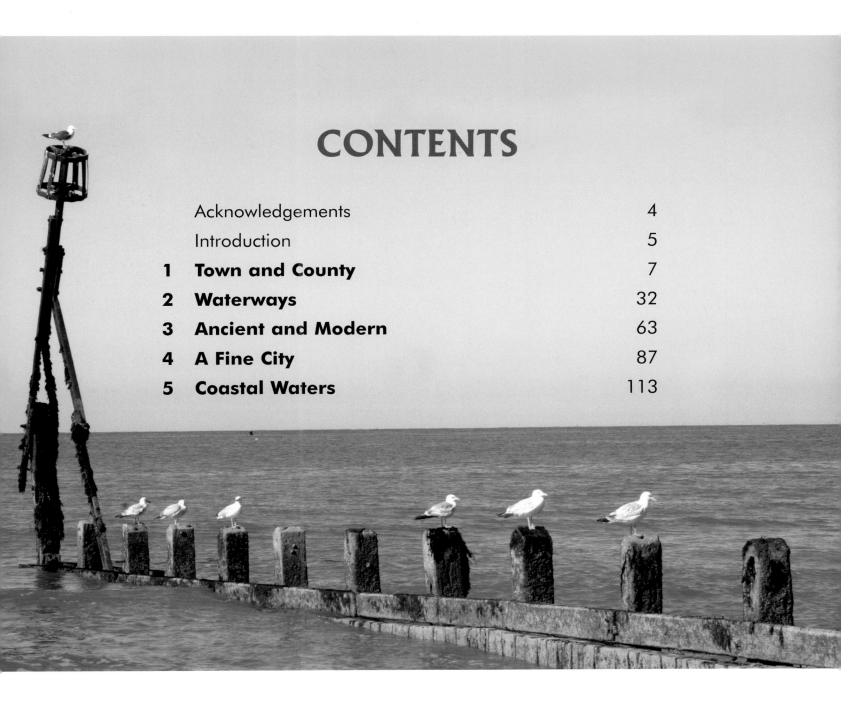

CONTENTS

ACKNOWLEDGEMENTS

I am deeply indebted to Air UK; Battle of Britain Memorial Flight; Karen Binaccioni (for her patience and design expertise once again); Tim Crocker, Norwich City Council; Lisa Cutter, Great Yarmouth Racecourse; Major Eadie, OC, and Captain Steve Graham, 669 Regiment, Army Air Corps, Wattisham; Andrew Hay, Office Facilities Manager, Norwich City Council: David Hunter, Fakenham Racecourse; KLM UK; Beverley Robertson; Maggie Secker of Radio Norfolk; Roy West; Zero Nine.

INTRODUCTION

Norfolk never changes. Or does it? Traditional trades like engineering, shoemaking, mustard milling and, to a large extent, chocolate and cracker biscuit manufacture have almost vanished, while actors, playwrights and even ex Prime Ministers have made Norfolk their second home or their home from home. Pleasure cruisers still ply the inland waterways but deep-sea fishing, once a major industry in the region, has largely disappeared and oil and gas platforms have sprung up in their wake. Sailors are still respectful of the treacherous coastal waters of the North Sea, once the graveyard for many unfortunate vessels where lifeboatmen like Henry Blogg rescued seafarers by the score. Fortitude in all weathers is axiomatic and now helicopter crews and the RNLI have the latest technology to support their brave resolve.

Norfolk people probably take the county's rich history and highly arable land with its inland waterways and coastline teeming with bird-life for granted but its wide-open spaces have been fought over for centuries. Time and again the invaders were repelled or they won the day and came to stay. Now day-trippers from near and far and holidaymakers from overseas have replaced the warlike hordes of Scandinavia who added old Norse to the broad Norfolk dialect and introduced many names to the geography of the region. Talking of geography, where else could you visit California and Ostend in the same afternoon?

What does this county signify to most people? Norfolk dumplings, wheat, beet, Big Sky, Breckland, Broadland, beaches, bloaters, boats and barley. Creeks, crab, cockles, samphire, shrimp. Nelson, Paston, Cavell, Cotman, Crome. Canaries, castles, cathedrals, cliffs, cottages, keeps. Flint, flat fields, gas fields, turkey farms, wind farms, stately homes, holiday homes, sand dunes and summers by the sea. Mustard, marshland, rivers, villages, vistas, ferrys, wherrys, windmills, whelks, waterways, wildfowl, walks and way beyond.

Norwich is at the hub. A magnificent cathedral and proud castle dominate the skyline. Viewed from the 206 feet high City Hall clock tower the city looks small and compact and it comes as a surprise to see that it is hemmed in on all sides by hills. Actually, the city appears to nestle in a bowl. During the Second World War this feature made locating the city difficult for enemy bomber crews but Norwich sadly did not escape widespread destruction on occasion.

Allied personnel stationed in the county came to love the area and some stayed to put down roots. Jackson Granholm was one of thousands who returned to the USA and spread the word that helps make Norwich and the county of Norfolk famous throughout the world. Granholm recalls: 'The great stone needle of the Norman cathedral of Norwich gave us a landmark from afar as we peeled off to land at Horsham St Faith… we could see it for miles in any direction and it… was an especially welcome sight – it told us we were safely home again.'

Murray Peden DFC QC, a Canadian wartime pilot whose classic autobiography, *A Thousand Shall Fall* is based partly on his time flying from Oulton, adjacent to Blickling Hall, and leisure time in Norwich, says: 'I have fond memories of the Castle Hotel in Norwich, although the secluded little green behind the cathedral nearby where Edith Cavell is at rest has also been by far the most indelible impression I have of the general area. I occasionally saw in the darkening sky the spire of the old cathedral looming off in the distance, usually as we swung on to an easterly heading just after take-off and made for the coast and the unfriendly stretches beyond. I never saw it without thinking of that wonderful brave woman sleeping in its shadow. We had read about her as kids when we were at school and I always had the greatest admiration for her courage. I read more about her as I grew up and used to remember, too, that she had spent many summer holidays at the coast at Cromer. And many times Cromer was our point of departure on operations.'

Ernie Frohloff, another Canadian stationed at Oulton, recalls: 'Life for the groundcrews was a daily routine of getting a maximum number of aircraft serviceable for the next op. Leisure time was spent in our favourite pubs and at the "large, modern NAAFI in Norwich". We had lunches of fresh crab on the cliffside at Sheringham and Cromer where we played golf but were warned never to try and retrieve a ball from the beach, as they were mined!'

Captain Ralph H. Elliott, an American pilot stationed at Rackheath just outside Norwich regularly sent letters home to his wife Vonny: 'We decided to go take a look around Great Yarmouth…The beaches are all closed off now with barbed wire and pillboxes…the beaches are mined…From Britannia Pier we walked south on the big, wide walk for several blocks. It was quite a resort area in peacetime…'

At Hunstanton, there is a memorial listing all those killed in the North Sea floods of 31 January 1953. It includes seventeen American airmen from RAF Sculthorpe.

Spring tides and waves whipped by high winds threaten vulnerable stretches of the seashore like a ravenous sea monster, which when hungry takes great bites out of crumbling cliffs and high-piled sand dunes with impunity. Marram grass only stabilises the dunes while the wooden groynes that zig-zag the shingle and sandy beaches cannot halt tide and time any more than Canute could. Erosion is everywhere. There are no motorways, and the pace of life is slower, but the county's rich heritage is under siege from developers as suburban and urban 'renewal' gain momentum. But then haven't opportunists consistently shaped our land? Since Roman times, land has slowly been reclaimed from marshland and coastal waters. Medieval peat digging produced the thirty shallow freshwater lakes that became the Norfolk Broads.

In wartime, Americans loved the Norfolk Broads, as Ralph Elliott confirmed in a letter home: 'Today has been beautiful out, Vonny, just like summer almost… We've been figuring on whether or not to get a yacht for the summer and this afternoon we went to the Broads to see about a boat. There's about 200 miles of river around here to sail on and it's not far from here so that most any evening we could go up by bike. On a two-day pass we figure we could have a swell time with a 16 or 20-foot sailboat. After talking it over, the five of us have about decided to invest in a 3-bed, 24-foot yacht. It's going to cost us each about £2 a week but we figure it will be worth it just for the fun and relaxation.'

Elliott had to carefully explain what was meant by the 'Norfolk Broads' to stay out of trouble at home. Actually, it was a houseboat that they poled down the waterway and managed to anchor out in the Broads for the summer. In 1982 Ralph Elliott and his wife Yvonne returned and the same boat was still anchored out in the Broads in exactly the same place as they left it in 1945!

I owe allegiance to former flyers that flew from Norfolk. Corresponding with so many of them led me to researching and writing several books about these fine people. Flying the length and breadth of the county in aircraft and helicopters to photograph their bases and old haunts before they disappeared forever led to my earlier book *Echoes of East Anglia* and *Airs and Graces*. At the same time the opportunity was there for a long overdue portfolio of aerial and ground images of my county as a whole. This personal selection is the result.

Martin W. Bowman,
Norwich

TOWN AND COUNTY

Muckleborough selection

This is Diss

Long Stratton

Kimberley

Downham Market factory

Sunday service

Bypass surgery: Attleborough and A11

Cawston

Opposite: Hingham

Thorpe End

Wymondham at dusk

Bypassing
Wymondham

A day at
Fakenham races

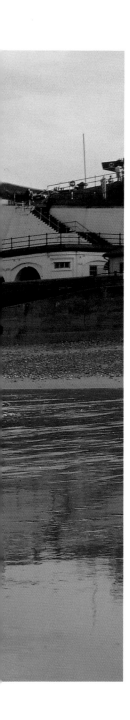

X marks the spot - Cromer

The Gem of the Norfolk coast - Cromer

Castle Acre

Binham Priory

Baconsthorpe Castle

Stalham Mill

Bircham Mill

'Windmills of Your Mind' at Weybourne

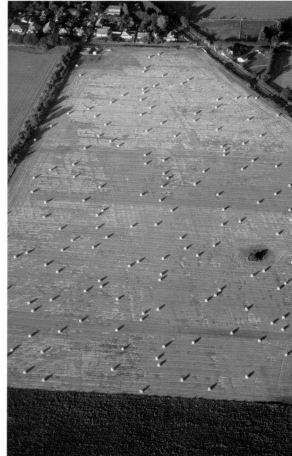

Eventide over Salhouse

Crop circles. Danish camp near Warham All Saints

Breckland flint

Peddars Way

Long shadows of autumn

Reap and sow

Harvest time

Bridleway to Mannington

March snow at Haveringland

Opposite: Dereham, snowbound

Red berries
at Redwings

Nelson Touch near Burnham

Poppy field at Rackheath

Quidenham

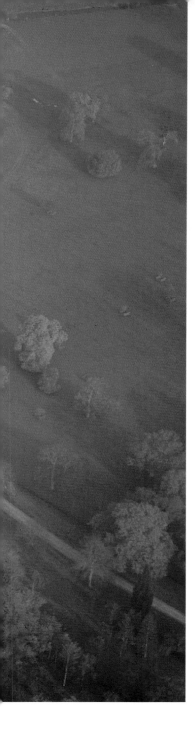

Humprey Repton's Masterpiece – Sheringham Park

Haydon

Shipdham Sunset

WATERWAYS

Straight and narrow near Lynn

King's Lynn quayside

Buoys will be buoys

Fleet's in at Lynn

Rory James

Ranworth Broad

The Point about Blakeney

Blickling Park

Stiffkey

Ranworth

Cranworth

Caravan idyll betwixt Brandiston and Buxton Heath

Opposite: Near How Hill

Ouse - west of King's Lynn

Whispering Reeds boathouse,
Hickling Broad

42

Norwich yacht station

The Blue Barge

Buxton Mill

Flour mill no more

Moorings

Foundry Bridge

Riverside at Dusk

Pulls Ferry

Wensum Vanguard

Night falls at Pulls Ferry

The *Albion*

St. Benet's Abbey and the black sail of the *Albion*

DUCK!

Cow Tower, Norwich

Potter Heigham

Airborne at Great Massingham

Hickling ducks

Clear to land at Blickling Lake?

Fritton Lake

Wroxham

Horning

Paddle steaming past the Ferry Inn at Horning

Bend in the River at Thorpe

Flotsam and jetsam

Beached

The Gangway

Time and tide

Making a splash at Cromer

Night falls

Nelson's other Column, Great Yarmouth

Opposite: Great Yarmouth

Crane your neck through for this view

Safe haven at Yarmouth

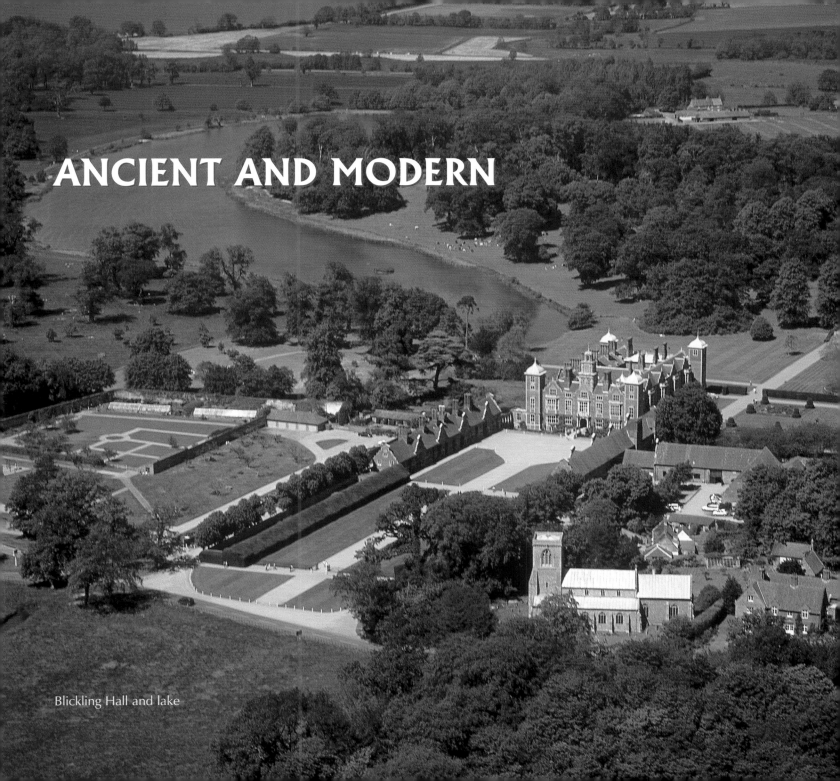

ANCIENT AND MODERN

Blickling Hall and lake

Blickling Hall

Blickling Hall and lake
The Buckinghamshire Arms, Blickling

Felbrigg Hall - built in the seventeenth century

Oxburgh Hall

To the Manor born
near Barsham

Holkham Hall

Helhoughton Hall

Helhoughton Hall and the Raynhams

How Hill
Eel Cutter's Cottage, How Hill

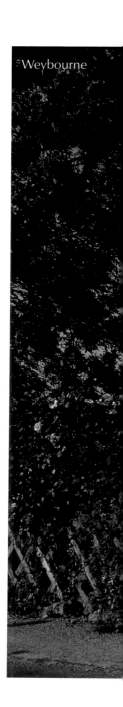

City cottage, Norwich

City shopping, Norwich

74

City folk in their natural habitat, Norwich

St Mary's Plain, Norwich: Street Scene

Norwich: Car and cathedral

Spire in the snow

Cloistered
existence

78

Castle Keep takes a bough

Light fantastic

Time for
reflection

Forum folk

Norwich Union Marble Hall

Colegate

Union offices Surrey Street, Norwich

Ringing the changes around Chapel Field

A river runs through Norwich

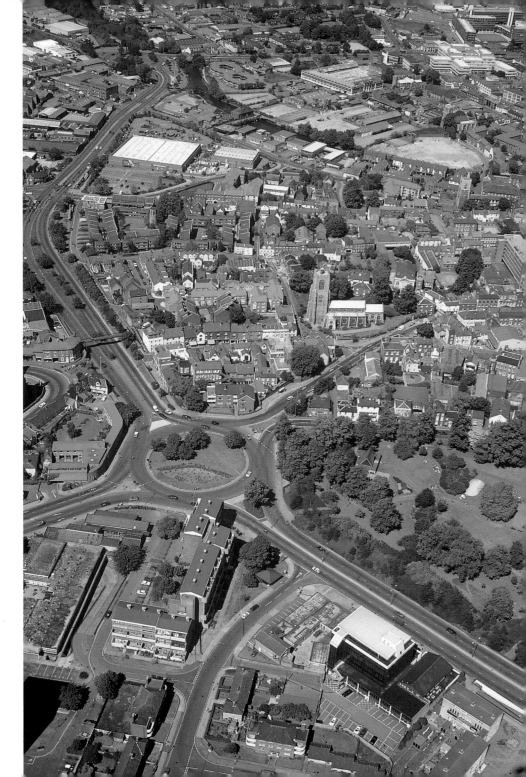

Norwich city centre

A FINE CITY

Running rings around St Johns

Elm Hill

Elm Hill's nursery slopes
in February snow

Captured on canvas - (two teas at the Britton's Arms Coffee House?)

Stripe me!

Market forces

City lights

Yes we have no bananas

Trading places

92

Aspiring to greatness

Walking the Walk

Cathedral Close

St Johns at dusk

Edith

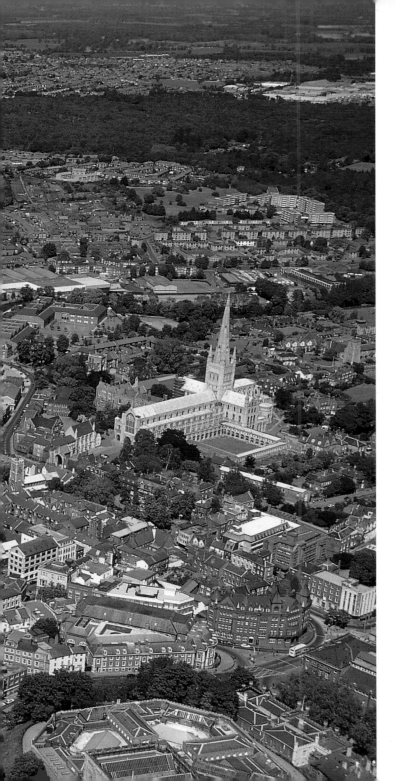

Fine façades

Giving way in Westwick Street

Opposite: Norwich in June

Road, River and Rail

Churchgoers

Fine Vintage...

...Fine City

Mile Cross

Behind these walls at Norwich Prison

Breaking cloud over Bowthorpe

White Woman Lane

The Boundary

Today Mousehold Heath tomorrow the Cresta Run?

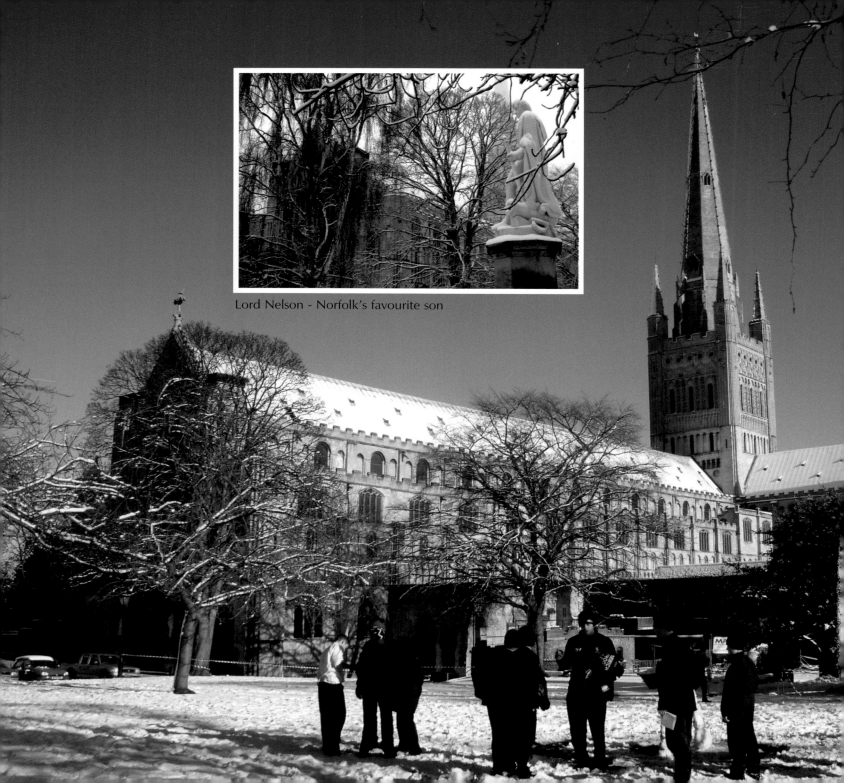

Lord Nelson - Norfolk's favourite son

In the bleak midwinter

Opposite: Cathedral choir?

London Street

Opposite: Anchors Quay

Tombland

Tombland Alley

Millennium Plain

Waterworks Road

Drayton

COASTAL WATERS

Sea spray

You've been warned!

Wells waterfront

Cromer cliffs

Wells-next-the sea. Where else?

Hunstanton Cliffs

Hunstanton Light through the ruins

Sweeping the beaches

Hunstanton Beach

Hoops at Happisburgh. Hard to believe the lighthouse was built in 1791

Opposite: The road to nowhere from Happisburgh

Cromer and the
Royal Cromer Golf
Club

View with a room

120

Tractor boys

Amanda Ann at Overstrand

Henry

Red Lion

Cley-next-the sea

Made in Cley

Ropes and anchors

Shingle floodwater bank, Gramborough Hill,
Salthouse

Strangers on the Shore at Sheringham

Great Yarmouth

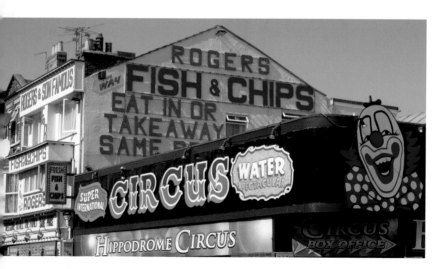

Red nose day

'I've looked at clouds from both sides now...'
Scroby Sands in-bound from Holland

Pier of the Realm

Britannia Pier and Theatre Great Yarmouth

Winter Gardens in November. Brrrrh!

Winter Gardens warming up?

Wellington meets Waterloo

Yarmouth jetty

The far pavilions: Cromer

Cromer crabs

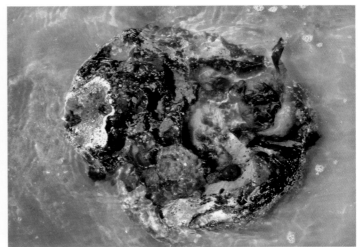

Seaweed and stones

Bed and Breakfast

Silver dream machines on the Seafront's Golden Mile

The sport of kings at Great Yarmouth

Racing fraternity

Racing certainty?

Bronze beach

Opposite: Low tide

Sun, sea and sand

Groyne strain

Panning for gold

End of the Pier Show at Cromer

Sunset over Breckland